# In Flow With Grace
**a poetic collection by Rawle Iam James**

It matters not if you can see my Love
for my Love is the hope in us all.
It matters not if you can feel my Love
for my Love beats in the hearts of all.

COPYRIGHT © 2019, Rawle Iam James

**Book Title: In Flow With Grace**
**Sub-Title: a poetic collection**
**Author: Rawle Iam James**

ALL RIGHTS RESERVED. Alesia Publishing and its authors recognize all information, including the material in these sacred texts, comes from the collective consciousness. However, no part of this book may be reproduced or transmitted in any form or by any means, electronic or mechanical, including photocopying, recording, or by any information storage and retrieval system without express written permission by the author. Any unauthorized reprint or use of this material is prohibited.

The intent of the author is only to offer information of a general nature for your general use and well-being.

Cover Art *Mother's Heart*: Harris Ian James
Back Cover and Inside Pages: Pamela Lynch
Publisher and Editor: Pamela Lynch, Alesia Publishing

ISBN: 978-1-9990394-4-8

# DEDICATIONS

### Agnes 'Mom' Toppin
You are our family trailblazer and the most courageous woman I know. Your sacrifice of leaving Trinidad and Tobago, and your three young boys, opened doors of opportunity for us all. This was both inspiring and the foundational factor to all that we have achieved in life. You are a shining example of perseverance and never giving up. Mom, you are a constant presence in our lives and our Heroine. We (Rawle, Jason, Harvard and Melissa) are the sons and daughter of Agnes Nina (James) Toppin. We Love You Mom.

### Neville 'Pops' James
What an interesting, purposeful, challenging and inspiring experience we choose to walk Pops. You are the original superhero to three little boys who grew into men who house many of your qualities and strengths. As I write these words, I hold no regrets. We will always have our Baja adventure where during the front end of that trip, you encountered a confronting son wanting answers. At the back end was a son connecting with his father and witnessing why he was our superman. You will forever be in the hearts and minds of your boys, Rawle, Jason and Harvard. We are the sons of Neville Winston James. We Love You Pops.

# TABLE OF CONTENTS

| | |
|---|---:|
| DEDICATIONS | iii |
| ACKNOWLEDGEMENTS | vi |
| MOTHER'S HEART | vii |
| IN THEIR WORDS | viii |
| FOREWORD | xii |
| PREFACE | xiv |
| IN MY WORDS 1 of 30 | 1-77 |
| EPILOGUE | 78 |
| TITLES | 80 |
| A FINAL WORD | 82 |
| ABOUT THE AUTHOR | 85 |

# ACKNOWLEDGEMENTS

*My siblings:*
Jason James
Harvard James
Melissa Williams

*The mothers of my children:*
Chera Harris
Tanya Kotsopoulos

*My children:*
Harris Ian James
Zen Ian Kotsopoulos-James
Irie Agnes Kotsopoulos-James

To my ancestors and the poets
who came before.

*a poetic collection*

The book cover is called *Mother's Heart* which depicts the balance of the giver of life as she nurtures the essence of our being and Love. Mother's Heart is an invitation for us to be strong in our truth like a tree without judgement. She takes no sides as her permanence is in all seasons. The fruit born of the tree are experiences of light and dark that foster our strength for growth that is rooted firmly in her Love.

The book cover beautifully captured by my son and artist, Harris Ian James, is called *Mother's Heart*.

# IN THEIR WORDS

The youthful soul can be wise, too. The sun and their stars have their time to each present their light to our eYes. Some hate the sun while others cry when she doesn't visit. Many dream of the beauty of the stars and fail to appreciate the beauty that lies in between their absence. But there live those special gems who choose to drink of the full cup of life's gift. To drink it all. The juice plus the dregs of pulp squeezed into the cup. For us, we are blessed to have watched Rawle visit our life experience. To witness one who blesses sadness with the same gratitude as he does joy. Tears with the same love as laughter. We are witness to a man who has said thank you to the Universe's gift of life. A life truly lived and loved for all it brings. Without knowing, he dissolves the binary of good and bad into the nothingness they are by simply being. It is with this great pleasure that we are honoured to be praising the poetry of a vessel of the Universe. One that has accepted his true greatness. The greatness of 'being' in all of life's mysteries.

*with Love,*
*Glory's Parents*
*Trophy Ewila and Mundia (Dia) Kabunda*

*a poetic collection*

Rawle challenges you with a provocation: "It stirs within!" Just like that, you enter the manifesto of a talented and charismatic leader who is a lover of words. This book is full of considerations—ways to open oneself to the power held within. Even more so, though, it is full of observations.

Moments distilled for the reader to hold closely. To look at under the light. To be one with when the world is dragging you down to the mud. In this collection of poems, Rawle uses refrain like a master performance poet, calling on the repetition known in song and incantations.

This is also a book of love, in all of its manifestations. At the heart of this man and this body of work is a deep connection to the sensual self. The part we don't often value in ourselves, the part where "vulnerability is king."

Thank you to Rawle for showing the world the power of self-acceptance, unashamed love for personal history and identity in the face of marginalization, and above all, how to be gentle with oneself. You are a true gem, Rawle. We are so lucky to walk along this path with you.

— *by Erin Scott*

I first met Rawle at an Inspired Word Café (IWC) event in 2013. The brainchild of Rawle, IWC is an open mic that has turned into a non-profit, local institution in the Kelowna arts scene. I went to support a teacher and mentor of mine, Sonnet L'Abbe, who was reading that night. The event to me seemed like what white, conservative Christian people love to call "new age," whatever that means. As a young university student who knew very little of community work, or what poetry can mean locally, I was highly critical of the event. I later called it weird. I was short-sighted and arrogant, but there was a bunch of old hippies doing like 1960's versions of gospel songs and replaced the word 'God' with 'creator' or 'mother earth' and that sort of thing—it *was* a bit weird. What I didn't know then was that weird was good. Weird was welcoming. Being welcomed, at first, always feels weird. That must be an evolutionary tactic.

When I came back to IWC in the fall of 2015, a performance poet trying to find the community I had failed to create myself, I felt very different. I was welcomed and upheld. I still found the whole thing a bit odd, but only because it was a different experience of poetry than I had ever had. I was older, and slightly wiser, and knew better this time (I hoped). Different,

*a poetic collection*

especially regarding poetry, is good. Rawle cultivated a poetry community in Kelowna that loves, interrupts, burps, snores, and shakes their knees. He created a space where people can come to share under the banner of poetry. The book you are about to read continues this ethos and his work. It isn't like the other books of poems you have read because Rawle is different than other men you have known. Whatever your relationship to poetry, the world or yourself, this book welcomes you into its open arms. It reminds you that you are beautiful because you are. Like Walt Whitman, Rawle gives you his body, which is also the universe, which is also pages between a cover, which is also a bike lock. His verses are biblical, but the only thing he asks of your soul or your life is that you love yourself. He inspires you to take a glass from the top shelf, and to love the shape of that shirt you hate because that shape is your shape. As in life, he invites you to look for yourself and to be gentle no matter what you find.

Like the man who wrote it, this book is boisterous, and good-vague (a wall with a rainbow of buckets of paint to throw), and filled with wisdom. Enjoy.

— *by Cole Mash*

# FOREWORD

What to say about Rawle and his works? Rawle's words have a way of inviting the reader or listener to share in some of his most intimate moments of raw thoughts and emotions. We ache for him and with him, stand with him, cheer with him, cry with him, and simply enjoy the moment with him. The thing I have always loved most about Rawle's poetry is the sense of connection it evokes, with Rawle himself and with all humankind.

Rawle's love flows out of his writing, and if you have the pleasure of hearing him recite his poetry, the impact is that much greater. Rawle's poetry is more than a lovefest of tender emotion, though! He will challenge you, to stand for yourself and your fellow man, to know and be your truest, most authentic self, to be present to and savour each moment.

*a poetic collection*

Traveller, poet, father, brother, son, friend, lover, guide, mentor. Rawle is many things to many people, but ultimately, he is simply...human. Like the rest of us. Whether you know Rawle personally and have been enjoying his poetry for years, or have randomly picked up this book and have no idea what you're about to dive into, I hope you enjoy the experience and hear this dear man's heart beating for you, simply because you are.

by Larelle M. Anderson

# PREFACE

People in my circle have asked, "Why are you writing this book?"

I have pondered this same question. My truth is, I believe poetry is meant to be shared. Its words are like endorphins that carries a tremendous internal and primal need for emotional expression that can bring us into grace with life.

Poetry showed up at my doorstep ten years ago when I was a teacher, and from that moment, it has been and continues to be, a blessing in my life. Of the seventy or so pieces I have penned, I can count on one hand the poems that I intentionally sat down to write. I am sure that like other artists, I receive downloads from my Lover, the Universe. We are in partnership, and she provides structured thoughts. It is my job to capture them. If it isn't, I believe the idea goes to the next possible aspirant. There are times I can feel the words coming. It's like an itch that cannot be scratched and the only relief is to put pen to paper.

Once captured, my part of the partnership is fulfilled by adding words based on my perception of self and life.

*a poetic collection*

This is my second book of poetry. It is a collection of poems that look at a variety of subjects that embrace our human experience through my perspective. It is my truth and not the truth. I am not invested one way or the other in whether *In Flow with Grace* is accepted or not accepted. That is a choice I leave to you. I hold no expectations for the potential reader except one—Love and know thyself. *In Flow with Grace* is my invitation to you, to step with the beauty and vulnerability of your own grace and beauty.

So, why did I write *In Flow with Grace*? On a more complex level, this poetry book is part of my contribution to uplifting our human consciousness. It's part ego, it's part legacy for my kids, and it's part 'My Love for you.' Whatever my reasoning for this book, only you can decide how it will serve you. Again, that is a choice I leave to you. Know you are Love.

Yes, I believe poetry is meant to be shared. Its words are like endorphins that carries a tremendous internal and primal need for emotional expression that can bring us into grace with life.

"Be gentle with yourself so you can be gentle with others." — *Rawle Iam James*

*In flow with* GRACE

*a poetic collection*

## 1 of 30

It matters not that we walk together for me to Love you
for my Love reflects Spirit.

It matters not if you can see my Love
for my Love is the hope in us all.

It matters not if you can hear my Love
for my Love is the sound that echoes eternal life.

It matters not if you can feel my Love
for my Love beats in the hearts of all.

It matters not if you know the touch of my Love
for my Love is the inhaled breath that is Life.

It matters not if you know of my Love
for my Love lives now and in all the days to come.

It matters not anything
for my Love for you is everything.

## 2 of 30

It was a cold and snowy day. The kind of day when the weather reflected the unpredictability of what was. I was lost in the sea of my attention, surrounded in a fog that hosted the demons of torment. Then out of nowhere, I heard the lighthouse of your voice; I could not see, but I felt your space within.

For too long, I had been trapped as a victim in the echoes of my mind. Venom coursed through my veins as toxic words fumbled with each other while impatiently waiting to be spewed. I was consumed by my victim's cry—my body slammed in anguish and battered from years of being lost and blinded by rage.

I straddled the thin between here and there as I swirled in my hangover of grief.

My arms acted like a cane that swayed side to side gingerly searching for a lifeline as I prayed that hope would shelter me from the turmoil of my memories. My mind was a distorted canvas of vibrant colours that housed the whirlwinds of chaos as I stood fully exposed at the crossroads of discomfort.

And for a moment, my heart forgot its purpose and skipped beats as tears flooded its chambers with the waters of inevitability. In that same moment, your voice was an invitation to the door of my rebirth. I was cocooned in the placenta of the unknown as dark clouds rained the numbness of sadness; like a deer in the headlights, I stood paralyzed unable to run from the fight.

My suffering had reached its boiling point from years of piling one-sided perception beneath the canopy of my forest. Psychosis or the burning bush, either way, your voice echoed from the valley of my shadow as a lifeline to the madness of that moment.

a voice I knew—a voice I know

The tenor of your words was like a sunset backdrop in the eYe of my storm. A gift from the depths that provided a force-field protecting my battered soul as waves gently crashed over me. Each serving as a reminder to the Spirit I am.

Caught in the intersectionality of the seconds, space was an illusion of linear time, and I was an unbalanced hiccup of hindsight awaiting an audience. The gentleness of your voice revealed wonders to my discomfort. I was still unsure of how or why but unknowingly the process of shedding my old skin of suffering had begun.

There is a beginning—an end to all life. My dash is my vault of wisdom to where my experiences are deposited and insight awaits withdrawal. It also houses your voice as a reminder that the light cannot exist without the dark. I am but one drop in an ocean of drops. I am here now to experience all; otherwise, this journey would be pointless and, quite frankly, boring.

So, until further notice, I'm celebrating every damn thing.

## 3 of 30

She is patient with time and expects nothing, for she knows nothing happens without a choice and in the right time.

She simply holds space to offer a hand for when I fall or a shoulder for tears to waterfall.

She cloaked my inner child with her unwavering spirit, but my foolish pride had me trapped in the fog of insensitivity that just for a moment allowed her beauty to be absent.

For only in the constant echoing of doubt did I question her resolve.

For you see, her beauty is her strength and her strength is beauty.

And as I stood at the threshold hesitating at the roads that lay before feeling alone and abandoned, I was conflicted by which path to take. I looked for courage void of fear as I searched both high and low for the strength of character that lingered in the chasm of right and left brain thinking.

Hoping that my choice this time would remove the rose coloured glasses that flooded me with ego's lust for balance between ignorance and blinded intelligence.

She is the unspoken whisper that floats upon the winds.
The shy slant of her eYes, hints of untamed playfulness.
The slight tilt of her head highlights her flowing braided hair and the way it partially covers her crescent moon smile.
For reasons beyond my understanding, her beauty shone like never before.

And as I stood trembling at the doorway of discomfort, she gently took my hand and placed it upon her heart.
And without an uttered word, she reminded me of the flame that burns within.
In that moment, her strength was her beauty for her beauty transcended the moment and appeared as a multitude of orchestrated thoughts.

Once again, I embraced her beauty to silent my own will.
I accepted her feminine wiles, which unfolded beneath my feet as solid ground.

And if I had the audacity to breathe in the particles of her beauty—my lungs would forever be filled!
My thirst forever quenched!

She invited me into my own vulnerability to see the strength of my own beauty.
Together we floated on a bed of water lilies on a river of her tears with only imagination as our guide as our souls frolicked and pranced in a state of content.

She once again reminded me that alone is a construct designed to blind self.
And as the days' light crept closer to revealing the nights' secrets, I safely cocooned my soul into her beauty, to dream dreams of shooting stars that lit up our souls' playground.
We fell with the sands of time witnessing time itself stand still.
We are reborn into our wild and free selves to dance for the sake of the dance succulently under the stars by the light of the pale moon.

For you see, her beauty is her strength and her strength is beauty.

It stirs within!
That which cannot be seen nor felt.
One with my true nature that's in grace flowing from spirit.
Every breath a connection to that which cannot be seen nor felt.
For there is no separation, God knows God.

I am the creative design that is conscious thought.
Here to experience all experiences in this ripple that is space and time.
Collapsed and folded from the agreement of my Love pulsates the understanding of me.

I am a construct of stardust.
A thought woven from the golden thread of life.
Within the wall lining of my cells lays the insanity of the nothingness that forged everything.
I blinked into existence my forest of discomfort for where the seeds of change take root to tower and shade my fears.
Spirit propels me forward on big blue as each moment a reward—a step closer to the state of nothing.

Death is only an illusion in my ego's mind as my heart quickens in anticipation of that which cannot be seen or felt.

Gratitude fills my lungs to the truth that all things are truth.
For I am a creation of that which cannot be seen or felt.

Infinity my trinity.

I am the father.
I am my son.
I am mother.

Three wisdoms that arouse my every breath to the fullest of life's capacity.
Each exhale a single drop into an ocean of drops enticing the winds
to soothe and gently blow the trees of my forest into a dance of unity.

I only need to look within my memory bank for wisdom.
For her existence was, is, constant.
She is my companion.

*In flow with* GRACE

I need not look to the heavens for this truth is placed in the hearts of all.
It matters not be it dynasty or faith for spirit's birthright is to be.
So here in flesh I am.
Each inhale and exhale unlocks that which cannot be seen nor felt.

Feeling whole, I flow within the good graces of the Universe.
I have learned that loving self is a practice of patience.
For patience brings me closer to embracing my Nirvana.
And my Nirvana is not after I have taken my last breath.
My Nirvana is an activity for the living.
As I blink into existence everything from the nothingness
which cannot be seen nor felt.

I've gone around.

I've come around.

I'm everything and nothing.

The particles of space that makes up everything,

the reality of illusion.

In to me I see!

In to you I feel!

The emptiness that is everything and nothing

separation from all things only to exist in my ego's eYe.

The duality of wholeness is oneness insanity.

I explore the inner depth that is my mind.

I see me, observing me, standing at the portal.

Seeing me, eYeing self in the mind's trap that is my karma.

Happiness or pain both anchors to my growth.

Both manifested from my choices.

My deeds.

I no longer seek answers to what is everything and nothing.

For we flow in all things.

We are all things.

I am that I am.

tumble-tumble
my thoughts forever tumble

forward
bouncing from hope to wish
and back to the ethers
do my thoughts hope
are my hopes a wish
a wish of formulated ideas
sprouting from the soil
of undreamt dreams
becoming a garden that enriches
the art of my soul
fruitful
to the imagination of my inner child

tumble-tumble
like a child
always forward
soulfully playing with possibilities
my thoughts journey
from my heart's eYe
fuelling the dreams and hopes
that feeds imagination's life
words that forever tumble
forward
wishing upon planted seeds
that wills imagination's hope

i am in a dream

of my soul dreaming of tomorrow
as voices echo lucid thoughts of wisdom that tunnels through
the portal of my mind
i move with ease from synapse to synapse
igniting livid flows that spark the wild sanity of my truth

in a blink
i steal from future moments that knock me into a meditative trance
i capture the swirling winds that carry the seeds of life
rainbows arc between duality's anchors Love and Fear
as thought and experience balance in painted streams of space
that houses the consciousness of God

i am awakened
buried in this dream of a cloaked and unfinished story
page by page I unveil the plot of an expanded idea that is me
within arm's reach of pencil and eraser I pen a manifest
of a soul contract made of my past, present, and future
the truth of my truth
the idea that is me at the centre of consciousness
in the vast blackness of the universe between
the particles of space that is neither here nor far

## 8 of 30

I am a wild child
free to daydream of dragonflies that leap lightly upon the waters
Sunflowers tower towards the sun mesmerized
by a slow and attentive kiss by a butterfly.

Particles sway in rhythm
to a gentle yet exotic dance with the trees
The cold north wind serenades the leaves from their branches
to a fall of admiration within the opus of life.

I am the meadow boasting
loudly with wild colours of purple and yellow
The sun coaxes flowers to release their seeds of change

that populate and inspire the minds and souls of poets.
The sweet fragrance
of jasmine and lavender electrify the air
stimulating the philosopher's heart with repeated hopes that power
the constructive revolutionary force of a generation.

I stand on the banks of the river
skipping rocks upon the waters of life.
Each jump serves as a reminder to be present and humble
as my soul reconnects to its wild and free nature
under a pillow of clouds of Mother's love.

Rhapsody in choice is wrapped in a celestial energy wave that sways back and forth on life's pendulum
The sentiment of chaos muddies the waters into a whirlpool of evolutionary sweat that drives both mediocrity and excellence

Greatness swells within as a symphony of knowledge and wisdom
God's tears fall from grace and gather to embrace my swim against ego's will

Doubts persist with each conflicted stroke while my equilibrium foregoes the insanity of the greater fool
I am the hamster running back and forth aimlessly on the teeter totters of the monkey brain

Trapped like bobbing buoys in the deep dark abyss treading the waters of uncertainty of an imagined barrier
Fighting the demons of despair and suspicion with my sword and armour of Love

I seek the path of the high road for that is where I am

told greatness lays
But that little voice within says be warned for each step is a treasure chest and land mine of experiences wrapped in the magician's illusion of good and bad

The insanity of infinity's loop has taught me that I am worthy to walk the middle ground
I no longer choose to hitch my wagon to ride the highs of the high
or the lows of the low

And like the Phoenix who rose from the ashes I too ascend from the depths of my flames to new heights
I am a balanced sage of my masculine energies knowing my feminine is only a thought away

For in this now choice awakes and my soul opens to the Love that has always dwelled within
I cast away the shadows of doubt as I accept the infinite finite that I am

For death's grace is a reflection of my mortality
I am the middle secure in the stillness of the Rhapsody in Choice

This rhapsody of words is a yawn that I hope will take you on a celestial journey to where love invites you to go beyond imagination. You see, she took my hand and, in an instant, we were transported to the emptiness of the beginning. We travelled through black holes and wormholes, linked only by moments. Back to when the playground of time and space was nothing but a thought. Surfing galactic waves as we were slingshot around the sun, eYes wide open to the lucid adventures of duality's realm.

Gravity ripped us into these carbon-based bodies of pleasure and pain with an intensity that brought us forth crying to the equinox of change. Thirty kilometres per second. One heartbeat expanding everywhere in all places. Out of the dark, light spewed purpose into the fertile void bringing forth my lover's child. Truth by design, we created stories of evolution to make sense of the chaos. If only to find our place in the vastness. The tears of my lover washed over me to baptize the rhythm that propels life forward on this sixth rock to the sun.

Her Love is complete and allows us to hang our heads as we fight our soul's purpose. Sitting at the intersection of ignorance and discomfort, we are trapped in the illusion of permanence as we swim in the dark conflict of our mind. Our patiences and tolerances stretch beyond their elasticity as we await their snap back to sanity. The invisible energy that drove our adventurous spirit out of the caves is the same energy of self-realization that fuels our fears of the unknown. It is in the uneasiness of knowing that leads to questions that cannot be answered. This is a battle that wages within each living soul. We search high and low, to the four corners, stretching beyond the fringe to feel alive. But I was born from your breath to die. Death's value comes from time, yet one is guaranteed and the other is not. You closed a door in my mind while opening a window in my heart for wisdom's glow to shine. From a near distance, voices of generations past echo the cry: are we willing to lose everything in order to have everything? While in the same breath from a howling distance, the voices of tomorrow's souls whisper faint murmurings of a daydream. Are we willing to lose all that we value to value all?

And as the witching hour approaches, I fear the increasing seconds building to my lover's midnight. I pass through ignorance into the chamber of knowledge. And out of despair, I empty my cup of ego's water to quench my thirst of hunger and misery. Out of the perpetual fires of conscious souls, my temperance raises as the Phoenix silhouettes against the full moon's splendour. Shame and guilt challenged my night's work. But a new strength is derived from my Lover's light. Out of the murky waters of doubt, I walk into the sunshine of my redemption casting shades of worthiness. I have freed my mind's eYe of scarcity song to sing the chorus:
we all breathe the same air,
walk the same earth,
drink the same water.
We all come from woman,
and death will visit us all.

The Universe is my Lover, for all creation is the truth.

We are energy of infinite possibilities as the illusion of choice governs the construct of Us.

Our collective fears drive the insanity of answering bottomless questions.

Beyond the answers of philosophy, religion, or science.

Who is aware that I am thinking?

Listening as I ask the questions?

Who is the who listening?

Who am I?

Perception entertained humorously and freely as it witnesses my struggle with self.

All along knowing the answer to the question.

It is the asking of the question, in the pursuit of wisdom, that leads to answering these questions.

We become conscious to the consciousness that we are the questions and the answers.

For we manifest all.

## 12 of 30

I've dreamt of a life not yet lived that plays out in a wondrous tale of a movie starring my unborn self still tethered to a lucid wave of silence.

Out of the screaming silence, I appear fighting my broken-hearted self as ego tries to make sense of itself hiding in the corner.
I tremble and speed through the portal to nowhere as yesterday's psychedelic thoughts crash upon the shores of my untested soul.

I peel through a cocoon of experiences yet realized, looking to discard unwanted pains.
All the while my yet to be realized desires penetrate the heavens of my mind in a choreographed dance that triggers the illusion of my trinity.
Out of the contradiction, I appear as all things, not one thing.
Zigzagging the constant conflict of my inner self, I navigate the lens of stereotypes and hypocrisy of this broken-hearted walk.

I am the main character!
The central ingredient in the active sensory of my senses.
Time is the reaper claiming the arrows of life that open the scars to where the light of wisdom can shine.
In the eYe of my own storm, I wrestle with polarized thoughts that act as judge and jury intervening in the irrational insanity of my sanity.
Hurling at the speed of thought I am as a wild torrent of my alter ego's madness trying to make sense of the worthiness dance.
Bam! I find myself an expansion of unknown perceptions and, in a blink, I crash upon the shores of my battered body.

Confused in my stubbornness, I fight through the dark matter that blinds the madness as I succumb to gravity falling through the empty vastness of quiet.
In a painted landscape of possible, I play hide and seek with love and fear in the stream of space at odds with itself.
The past, present and future me flows like a river flooding my dreams with rainbows that serenade paraded clouds with arcing smiles that spotlight the anchors of duality.

Oh, the relief felt when you are a storm of brewing thoughts clinging to the strings of matter that is neither near nor far.

All that I am is truth for no temple or writings alone defines my compassion.

Pain, choice, kindness, the cornerstones of my broken-hearted walk.

Each breath a reconciliation with choices made.

Each breath takes me closer to everything and nothing of my warrior's soul.

I am my broken-hearted walk!

## 13 of 30

Lovers embraced the lazy stillness of the moment
while watching sea otters playing as they sat under the golden sky of an island sunset.
You see, she had ventured forth into the unknown
and guided me in my preparation to go beyond the sixth sense
fuelled by a lucid stream of dreams as we awaited the approaching dark.
I stood naked to the universe in full exhale of Mother's breath
as my understanding of me was stripped away.
I was beyond spoken words or expectations of the pending journey.
My surroundings humbled me as the silence carried my soul
to witness streaks of light that faded in and out of my altered state.

I stood upon the rocks of the shoreline as the receding water
wrestled itself back into the dark of night.
Swaying under a canopy of stars, my silhouette hand connected stars

like dots on a paper with bright magenta and violet.
While my lover swing-danced with the waves as they gently kissed the shore.
I twirled with arms touching the horizon and found myself front and centre to the fireworks of shooting stars and brightly lit fireflies that signatures the artist's touch.
Time was not a factor in this, the theatre of the universe, as my lover and I were drawn together to marvel and laugh at the silliness that seemed like reruns of the last moment.

As I hopscotched the multitude of rocks, I fell through a bottomless pit to where thought echoed the end of the beginning as my inhibitions were peeled away.
EYes wide open to the magnitude of another act in this celestial play,
as the silence of the moment orchestrated a symphony of unseen crickets that vocalized the rhythm between the waves' gentle kiss.
In the blink of the dark, my lover and I broke our solitude to venture in a moment of pure love that required no touch or words.
In a singular thought, I saw the beauty of creation upon her face

as she appeared as a window to my soul.

Like a light at the end of a tunnel,
I was drawn through her window only to find an infinite loop that brought me back to me.
In the softness of her eYes, I saw time stand still as all my desires patiently awaited her every breath which only intensified her beauty.
I stood with my arms wrapped around my lover and the moon as we witnessed tomorrow's dreams streaking by as visible light just waiting to be captured as answers to prayers.
The rhythmic beat of my heart echoed eternal hope as I sat in wonderment's awe under heavens' gate.
All my senses heightened, my psychedelic journey slowly blended back into illusion's reality.
Tears of gratitude flowed, my soul recharged, my heart full, my head a vault of thoughts of the journey experienced, all in alignment as my lover and I sat upon the sands welcoming the dawn's light.

Back into the sweet breath of Mother.

Stop. Rewind. Wait, I can't.
I am caught up in a loop of unwelcome thoughts nerve-rackingly biting my nails, trying to figure out what makes you tick. A boomerang of chain reaction thinking hits me upside my already battered head. I suspect from first breath the attempt to capture what cannot be captured is a peculiar dance with Pandora's box. The only thing constant is the impermanence of all things big and small, both prisoners to the essence and unchanging soul of each experience.

Fast forward. Wait. I can't.
How does one capture lightning in a bottle? Your bond is like the endless vertical that climbs beyond the heights of Everest. In a 360° turn, I search the horizon with eYes open, yet I cannot see the answers right in front of me. It's as if I am in the dark phantoms of the Mariana Trench. You are neither taste nor touch but the undefined space that binds the void into form.

*a poetic collection*

Pause! Wait. I can't.
You cannot be stopped, rewind, pause, fast forward or erased. You are not a video game where I'm playing out a scene trapped in a sandstorm of thoughts navigating blindly to the oasis of my soul.
You cannot be seen or felt, yet your mark is on every aspect of life. You are a wish made mostly when the turbulence of life hits to distract our focus to moments since passed, or moments yet to come.

Tick-tock! Tick-tock! I'm waiting.
We are not disjointed strangers. Our paths are interwoven, and my awareness transcends the conditioned Love of three-dimensional thinking. My own walls of fear no longer encase me as I try to escape that which is not guaranteed. We are two peas in a pod, like the air in my lungs that inspires life. I no longer take you for granted, as I embrace this moment knowing I am connected to all moments and all things. You are not invested in how you are spent. For you are present in all my choices.

Trapped
inside the dialogue of my mind
into the echoes of my past fables
dreaming illusions to come
searching for meaning in the despair
secretly longing to be authentic with self
yearning to be someone that I am already

Trapped
in the paradigm of conditioned Love
the daily grind herds us like cattle to the slaughter
perfecting the deadly sins of greed, envy and wrath
as society, schools, jobs, blinds critical thinking
ignorance stone walls my worthiness to the wisdom
that lays at the crossroads of the unconscious
consciousness

Trapped
in the hindering fog of chaos
a lucid dream of a dream just beyond arm's reach
walking the long-gated hall of hope
as the house of mirrors close chapters to my past
swaying on the pendulum eYes wide shut
put on trial to balance the apex of my battled soul

Alas
I am no longer trapped in the chaos of conditioned love
my straddle lies in the middle in the silence of my mind
my battered soul a reflection of life's journey
soaring to new heights of comfort and peace
knowing that my past choices are part of
the foundation to an authentic life
I drink of the waters of life with and in Love

I'm trying to breathe.
My nose wants to quit.
I'm yelling in quiet.
Body has forgotten its function.
A persistent morsel from a late-night conversation germinates in this dreamscape where there is no escape.
Is it subliminal lust neatly wrapped in a nightmare?

Is it fear playing ring around the roses in my mind questioning my respect for her—is this a weak moment?
An unspoken want from a friendship bound by platonic intimacy in the playground of the day walkers where all is possible.
His younger astral self to her feminine wiles as his midsummer eve flows as aged wine water-falling into a fountain of youth.
They both venture to where poets speak and singers swoon sounds of lust connected to the tone-deaf beat of denial.

Unspoken words appeared in captions above.
No promises of tomorrow.
Only pure human instinct of desire in this realm of where it all can seem surreal.
Up is wrong and down is right as they explore the forbidden fruit as juices oozed onto a canvas of unexpected excitement.
An ode to wet slow all in tongue kissing and uninhibited volcanic touches of raw carnal humanness!
I'm still trying to breathe.
Screw it. Let's Fuck!

## 17 of 30

The other night as I stood in the light rain conversing with my higher power.
In full practice of gratitude for being on the right side of the dirt and the day's experience.
This happened!

You know that feeling?
The feeling when you move your hand just right and you hit one singular raindrop.
In full flight—that feeling of exhilaration!
It's like being a kid on the swing, reaching the apex from a push.
And just before the descent,
there's a moment where you float in a suspended moment.

To fully let go!
Hands off the ropes.
Arms in perpendicular splendour.
That sensation of flying like a bird carefree as Spirit unplugged from the internal story.
Being connected to the innocence of the moment, in the existence of the moment.

I witness my own thoughts as they dissipate before my eYes.
Gravity and I dance a dance that seduces my imagination to be heroic in all future moments.
That state of oneness is what death might feel like.
No pain.
No knowing.
Just being!

I am in grace with the everything and nothing of the one raindrop.
Its magic is the same infinite jolt that births life as it propels me through the unknown.
From within the cryptic underbelly of the beast, it is revealed to me that the universe is my mind that crafts a series of suspended moments.
And as I blindly navigate through the fog of memories that shapes the illusion of my reality, my memories are frames of suspended moments.
Where front is back and back is a mirror playing in scrambled sequence in the theatre of conscience where time is neither space nor whole.

So, here I am.
Snatched back into my moment of gratitude.
Shaking my head in disbelief.
Questioning the lucid feelings that shape the reality within my world.
Either way, a glimpse experienced.
A glance into the power of the moment.
The oneness,
stillness,
chaotic,
playful,
noisy,
beautiful nature that is life.
Connecting me to the collective conscious that wraps me warmly in the blissful ignorance of knowing.

So, here I stand in the rain
knowing that feeling cannot be washed away.
As I free fall on my swing.
Back to zero.
Floating in a suspended moment that is everything and nothing.

To nigger or not to nigga?
Negro, please!
That was never the question.
For I've always been by definition, black.
So why is everyone hating on me!
The light cannot exist without me.
I do not breathe in derogatory nor do I bleed lazy.
Twisted context that advertised the anxieties of a false sense of self.
While conquering deeds, inhumane greed distracted from the inner symptoms, abnormal.
The sword made you master.
Whips and chains tools used to humble the flesh.
Words that taunt, cut to the bone as the forked tongue's saliva washed over the beast to soothe the savage.
Blinded intellect, misguided faith, kept the man a boy, woman a girl.

Today's descendants of the slave no longer under the yoke of oppression.
Many have fought the good fight so that the lost could rest in peace.

Each step forward brings us closer to our original glory, our rightful place.
The search for meaning takes time, as the deconstruction of mental slavery is a process.

Together we define this humanity through reclaiming the throne to self.
Our ancestors smile upon the future as together we reformat the power grid to release the guilt and shame that clouds truth.
No more waiting for tomorrow—for today is just as good to unshackle context's stain.
No longer victims to deceit, manipulation or coercion as we balance beliefs with the blinders of ignorance lifted.
So, no desegregating needed for I'm not a polite *N* or fools' slang.
I'm no junk bond or subprime so lose the derivatives and truly own all of me.

For I am defined by definition.
I am a friend. I'm a homey.
I am family. I am black embraced.
Civil by obedience.
Peaceful by nature.
I am black!
I am proud!
I'm not my nigga!
Nigger, I am.

## 19 of 30

I stand here, speechless.
Looking for the exit.
Scared shitless!
Too many minds in my head.
Look at them!
Their stares are like hot knives that peel away at my courage.
Exposing this scared little boy.

Here I stand at the foot of my Waterloo
as one thousand voices echo my fears.
I can't turn right!
Nowhere to go left!
Brick wall to my back!
Their "Let's get on with it," look in front of me.
What the hell was I thinking that I could write poetry?!
More importantly, that I have something worthy to say.
Or, that people would even want to hear my words.

I feel this knot in my stomach!
My mouth is dry.
Fuck, I think I'm going to die!
You know, that slow torturous death,

that 'Spanish Inquisition' type of shit?
Okay, that may be a bit extreme but where's that proverbial hole in the ground?
You know,
the one where you free fall endlessly into the shadows of doubt.

Don't get me wrong!
I wrote a poem.
Filled with words.
But fear has a hold of me.
It has control of my voice.
It tells me that all the work I have put into writing this piece,
the hours of practice,
memorizing,
standing before the mirror—up in the attic,
in the dead of summer,
as beads of sweat pour down my brow
and into my mouth like a river of confidence.
And now,
"Nothing!"
"Nothing," has me convinced that my nerves are to be feared.

Ya, ya, see that splatter on the brick wall?
Those hanging entrails of guilt and shame?
That's me from the last time!

The last time.
The last time.

The last time I end up splattered anywhere!
The last time I'm fearful of speaking my truth!

To bottle it up like a fine wine that grows in value over time.
Except for this poem, these words, like countless others only appreciated when spoken,
when shared!

Ignoring the energies of courage yet realized,
I'll be damned to have my truth screaming in silence.
As a white coat harvested it and gently placed it in a dish,
on a table with my other organs, from my own autopsy.
That can't be my FAITH!
Not me!

I'm so tired of this insanity!

Always afraid!
Scared of my own shadow.

If insanity is doing the same thing over and over,
well then,
I want a new insanity!
One where my vulnerability is king.
You know,
it's like screaming at the top of your lungs gripped with fear,
as you jump out of a plane for what seems like an eternity;
only to realize in the next moment,
why the fuck didn't I do this sooner?!

Okay, the mic.
That is my plane.
I just have to jump.
For all that I desire lays in the mic.
I just have to open my mouth and let it out.
Alright!
I got this!
I'm worthy to stand here.
I'm worthy to speak my truth.

if I am to die today
let me die a poet
pen in one hand
the other
love extended

if I am to die today
let my words ring truth
that they brought no harm
I said what I meant
meant what I said
spoke with Love

if I am to die today
let it be said
I walked gently
simple in grace
humble in body
back and forth on the path
of enlightened thought

if I am to die today
let me die
as my true nature
open heart
loving eYes
my karma neither good nor bad
I created past the illusion
to see we are one

if I am to die today
I'm happy
to have lived life
in every breath

## 21 of 30

When I look within me, I do not see black.
The essence that is me, freely travels the kaleidoscope of faint light that passes my mind's eye.
As I go beyond the invisible white fog of cloudy chaos that limits sight.
The ethos of my soul transcends the illusion of time and space, all pain, all suffering, all knowing.
I am the infinite vastness clinging to the illusion of the flesh, transported back to the feeling of my beginning.
I wrestle with the moment to go beyond my understanding of my body.
This name I answer to.

In a hypnotic gaze, I steer at the man in the mirror who's attempting to understand and not question the cascade of feelings that vexes.
My mind is a field of landmines scattered with memories, which are more glorified and treacherous than the actual event that created them.
In the soul of my soul, I am not a man, a son, a father, a lover.

*a poetic collection*

I am not short, tall, stocky nor slender.
I am not black, Muslim, Christian, Jew or gentile.
I am the particle circulating within the vastness of space that empties from the nothing to form the temple of my meat suit.
I am the many points of light guided by the forward notion that is life.
Riding upon shooting stars from experience to experience challenging choices not yet realized.
I am held captive by Patience for she is not my virtue.
As she disguises what I cannot see nor feel.

From dawn to dusk it all serves.
For how can we know light without dark.
The destructive creative flow that is God, the universe, looks through the eyes of the racist, the kind, the bigot, the meek, the banker, the housewife, the murdered, the starving, the wealthy, the servant.

When you look within you, what do you see?

What do you feel?

From the fringes of my consciousness, I pen this piece in hopes of inspiring an awakening from the distraction of life's b.s.

Deception cast a wide net over wisdom as we live in this fear-induced construct of ignorance.

I am caught up in a landslide of thoughts as I fight the downward tumble of energies in our midst today.

Debris of our human frailty fills the airwaves and suffocates the good that still exists in our hearts, as we rumble and toil towards making sense of who we are.

We live in a world where freedom is written and spoken, yet the stigma of colonialism holds the people in a vice grip of institutional slavery that favours one race over another.

While many remain imprisoned in glory days and others embrace a mindset that blankets the past with the morality of the present day.

I am not a nigger or my nigga.

As James Baldwin said in his talk, *Take This Hammer*, "It was an invented word. It was necessary to you. Not to me."

It reflected the fears that dwelled within to cover a false

sense of superiority through conquest and greed.
I am human! Black my walk!
Not a condemnation of race but a celebration of pigmentation.
I simply speak my truth, and my truth fears no investigation.
I pen these words as a free man of thought.
I am the many times' grandson of those who birthed the light from the dark.
My blood is the blood of kings and queens, the architects of great civilizations.
My ancestors experienced the good, the bad and the ugly.
And I am a proud descendant of those for whom the yoke of oppression goes past the Atlantic, Africa and Arabia,
To when we felt the lash of pharaohs and sultans.

Scattered to the four corners, our history hijacked, discredited and whited out to keep us disconnected and uninspired.
Families, culture and our own sense of self rewired.
Our men raped of their essence to be made boys; our women's virtues, valued as concubines for amusement.

While truth remained foreign to our minds, our tongues, our hearts.
Your spirit under a constant barrage of hell's fire.
Humanity denied.
Bodies beaten.
Crushed beyond recognition as pleasure derived from having the race beaten beyond the molecular makeup that binds all life.
Your daily bread barely enough to sustain life; never enough rest to honour the temple.
While praying on bloodstained knees waiting for the judgement day of the master's sins.

I call upon the spirit of my ancestors to guide my steps.
I honour the sacrifice made by standing up to injustices in hopes of fueling a revolution where no pound of flesh is required as penance.
I've looked within to Love, past the anger and hatred, to the wisdom welted upon your backs.
Hidden in the scarred and cracked lines in your faces from years in the sunbaked fields.
The thickened, rubber-like skin of your hands from centuries of making bricks and picking cotton that built wealth for others, but never your own.

In the chambers of my soul, I hear your voices echoing the call for the liberty that ties us in a single garment of destiny.
Your songs of freedom stayed constant as you carried this burden because it was yours to carry.
And as your ashes long returned to the earth to enrich growth.
The wind kicks up the dust of your bones as a reminder of that which cannot be broken as we await the awakening of our warrior's souls.

I issue a call to the four corners, to all my brothers and sisters.
Free your heart of fear to unshackle from the mental slavery of oppression.
Know the truth of Us!
The truth that We are a mighty people!
Know whose backs took the lash before you raise your hand against your own.
Know whose truth was denied before you speak with contempt and disrespect of our mothers and sisters.
Know the lives not lived before you want to end that of your brother.

The time has come for us to take our rightful place in the race.
Our lives have to matter to Us!
Our history, our true history, MUST matter to Us!
It is no longer us versus us or even us versus them.
Let us no longer be blind, deaf and dumb as we embrace a mindset that casts out the insanity of indifference.

We once dreamt of freedom.
It is time to awaken from the experience of mental entrapment and no longer be our own plantation masters.
We must be free within to live freely together.
Let us leave unto Caesar what is Caesar's and not attempt to fix what is not broken.
It is time to build anew that which values all life.
We are the fulfilment of prophecies that Bibi, Frederick, Malcolm, Martin, Angela, Shirley, Mandela, and Babu spoke of.
Let us all get right with our history, so we are not stuck in the hypocrisy of our history.

*a poetic collection*

For the time is upon us to walk with grace and dignity as we overcome and deliver on the promise of getting to the mountaintop.

It is said that the truth shall set you free, but only if one is open to the truth that binds us:
We all walk the same earth.
Breathe the same air.
Drink the same water.
We all come from woman.
And death will visit us all!

Let us not be colour blind but be human sighted.

## 23 of 30

Inspired by a man, wishing rod in hand.
A cup as bait at line's end casting for connection.
Just to be seen, to be loved.
Maybe a touch.
A bit of Hope.
Where are the people?
My people, my village.
Those who swim in conscious thought linked by the air we breathe.
This earth we call home.
Oh where, oh where, are my kind.

Our cities heart glows dimmer with each fading smile.
As we scurry around like a virus consumed by the fever of the rat race that drains our cup.
Lost in the forest of tall buildings.
Small parcels of nature's green.
Avenues lined with trees with the warmth of singled and stacked homes that invite a sense of wished peace amongst the concrete, glass, asphalt and cars.
Empty shells walking, riding, driving like zombies unable to smiles.
Oh where, oh where are my kind.

Are we so busy being busy?
Driven by the next text or Facebook update.
Conditioned to chase the fool's gold as we ignore the inner voice of our inner child that's blinded and deafened to the inner art void of concrete, glass, asphalt and cars.

My heart beats the drums of freedom.
My soul longs for nature unspoiled.
My body craves dirt underfoot.
To walk in blissful silence connected to all things.
My humanity.
Oh where, oh where, are my kind.

## 24 of 30

I'm going off the grid.
Grid off!
I'm grid'ing on to life.
Plotting a course of new.
Built on perplexes that vexes old usages.
My body turbines electricity.
Blazing a green path that shines a light of hope for our mother.

I've changed the grid within to survive the wilderness of my mind.
Stillness, conscious warriors, windmills that generate renewed hope.
No wish for a better tomorrow.
It exists now if we choose.

*a poetic collection*

Off the grid on the grid.
I'm plugging in!
Inhaling clean air as I see faces in the clouds.
Eating strawberries and raspberries.
Beets and watermelons from my backyard.
Hugging a tree.
Hugging ten times a day.
Minimum!
Feeling mother earth under foot.

I'm off the grid of fear and on the grid of love.
Grid on to life!

love me, you, us
intriguing use of words
relationship created around an idea
the conditioning of unconditional intent
bombarded by relentless thoughts
walking on the eggshells of potential's perception
loving you is a given
liking you is a conscious choice
trust isn't a knee jerk reaction
respect born from life's dress rehearsal
the mastery of living is ongoing
bound by gravity clutching to ego's playground
all the while fighting ego in search for answers
that lies at the bottom of the bottomless pit

i accept all of you by accepting all of me
in my heart's eYe i release my expectations
non judgmental in judging
for the practice of perfection lies in the imperfection
step by step embracing the contrast
in this world of my thoughts
i inhale air to sustain life
each exhaled carries a piece of me
as I return want and need polished and transformed
into me...you...us

## 26 of 30

In the resurrection of my ego,
I am conflicted and vexed at myself, the world, my creator.
I await absolution from capacity's anger.
Like the morning star, I fell from the mantle of salvation.
Gravity calling as failure loomed at the bottom of my fiery pit.

Last night, I cocooned myself swaddled in a blanket of bountiful intentions.
While under a cloudy night sky, I stood in your splendour as the midnight of your fullness approached to cast away my heavy thoughts of deliverance.
Wanting to cry but my tears would not flow this night which only further exacerbated my insecurities about my purpose.
Shadows came to life by your light to spotlight my impatience, as I trembled with anticipation of the pending ritual.

Tonight, by your grace, I stepped out of the mythic shadows to heal in spirit and body.
Letting go of the things that no longer served.

I was stripped naked before your judgement, heart-pounding suspicions of intent.
I drank sour wine that shocked my system into the sorrowful ways of a false kingdom. My mind filled with thoughts that crucified transformation conjuring choices that cause the effect of my own duality.
And like in a movie, the redemption song played as background music to the illusion of this event.
Unsure of what was real, my vulnerability appeared as authority preventing myself from being reborn from my soul's dance.

Body shivering as cold sweat trickling down my fingertips.
A new appreciation and benevolence for life rekindled.
I submitted.
Shedding the old trappings of my mind, as the love of my creator washed over me.
I rested for a moment.
Then, I picked myself up to rise out of what seemed like 40 days of discomfort into a new ascension of the warrior poet.

I am the embodiment of a new resolution here to honour the soul contract I made so long ago.
This is not a cross for one to carry for the burden is too heavy.
My convention is Love's entity guided by the angels.
I am one with spirit, gentle in mind, strong in body.
And so it is.
Until we embrace again in two fortnights.

we fight for peace
with trapped minds
guarded hearts
conditioned love
belligerent thoughts
inhumane choices
trade embargoes
unauthorized wars
one-sided laws
greed as right
eroding soil
polluted air
bloated bellies
thirst entrenched
homelessness
arrogant doctrines
suppressed rights
judgement in our blood
civil unrest
moral good
civilized torture
all along riding the rollercoaster of Einstein's insanity
singing our praises with guns, bullets, bombs

peace...peace...peace
i want me some Peace
we fight for peace
what an oxymoron
peace conjures up images of
open space
the void in silence
peace is the laughter of joyous children
embracing acceptance
the gentle sway of windblown trees
peace is the air we breathe
the waters we drink
the earth we walk
we fight for peace
enough fighting
shift for peace
let duality serve
to unleash our human splendour
live for peace like

*a poetic collection*


Bob Marley
Nelson Mandela
Martin Luther King
Rosa Parks
Cochise
Sitting Bull
Arafat
Mother Teresa
Harriett Tubman
Eleanor Roosevelt
John Lennon
Leo Tolstoy
Norm Chomsky
Steven Biko
Malcolm X
no more bullets, guns, bombs for we are evolution
i see you because i can see me
i lay down my tired arms
to rest in your grace
peace is me, you, us
Peace…Peace…Peace
i want me some peace

*In flow with* GRACE

## 28 of 30

I gaze upon a familiar face
refreshed conversation in friendship
ignites volcanic feelings to flow
ease in sharing
intellectual intimacy
emotional cleansing
one hour turns to four
in a blink
morphed into physical craving
mushroomed spiritual oneness
lost souls
reunited flames
no promises
no restrictions
void expectations
to dance the dance
as divine creation
we frolic in
surrender's bliss

## 29 of 30

Testing, testing, 1, 2, 3.
Is this thing on?
Are you listening?
It is my hope these words paint you a picture.
To inspire a melody in your mind as your heart dances to the tribal flow.
I invite you to listen closely.
The diversity that is our humanity can be found in our galleries, museums, libraries, science centres, halls of learning.
Since you are listening, let me pose the following.
What is culture? How does it define us?
Are you still with me?
Is it the art that hangs on walls?
The songs we sing?
The beating of drums that stir our ancestral energies.
The tribal dance of generations past.
Is it all that we have done?!
All that is to come?
Is life culture? Does it define us?

Now that I have your attention!
Our flow that vibes is culture.

Imagination constructs a creative life.
It forms our highest civility.
We are people of colour!
Black, red, white, yellow, brown.
We display our art with pride.
It is our earthly soul, joyously speaking.
A rainbow of culture blended as one.

Culture is
Expressive!
Creative!
Imaginative!
Perspective on life.
We are a tapestry of dance, song, music, art.
Words!
The human rainbow arcing from heart to heart.
Our collective inner voices are woven together.
It is an expression of our humanity.

Still with me?
Culture is family!
The root of our society.
From painting on cave walls to banging bones after the hunt.

We crave the outlet that fuels our creativity!
Fires the imagination!
It is a portal into our collective soul.
It gives license to express, protest, revolt, change and accept who we are.

Our internal art is our culture.
The rainbow dance of connection!
Culture is a window to look back and vision forward.
The door we peer through our evolutionary growth reflected in all that we are.
It is the dance of mind and body.
The air we breathe into song.
The thoughts that pen poetry.
Culture is our hope; our aspiration.
It speaks to the power of our spirit!

Before we depart, and I say thank you for listening,
Know this:
The collective creative energy that shapes our realities is our individual, collective expression of life's dance.
When we witness the inner art that defines our culture, we move closer to mindful acceptance of ourselves.
Culture is the sunrise and moonlight of our inner art.

*a poetic collection*

We sing the same songs with different voices.
We dance the same dance to different rhythms.
We write the same words spoken in different tongues.
We brush the same strokes that blossom in different colours.
Culture shows the soul of our community!
Our home!
It's how we define our uniqueness as One.
One Humanity!
One Art!
We are a rainbow of cultures.
Thank you.

## 30 of 30

Our hopes and dreams soar on the wings of the great eagle. As she lays witness to our collective spirit running wild and free like the mighty herds of buffalo and caribou. Wisdom sits on the branch of the old birch tree in the form of a Snowy Owl as she stands to watch perched with guarded optimism of what lies around the bend.

We are a people forged from the courage of the First Peoples who sought refuge fuelled by a vision quest of a new beginning. We stand on the backs of mighty people from many nations like the Inuit, Haida, Okanagan, Nakota, Algonquian, Innu. Whose sacrifice of living as strangers upon their own land laid the foundation for the French, British, Dutch, and Metis. Memories of their blood sweat and tears flow from all the waters as All our ancestors await our awakening. Their voices echo across every valley and inlet. From every shoreline to the highest mountaintops. Across the bountiful prairies, their spirit can be seen in the magnanimous colours of the seasons to remind the people of our rich heritage that embraces the good and the bad. Whispers carry seeds of change voiced like the cold fog breath of howling wolves whose cries haunt our memories of days gone by.

Today, I call forth a nation.

One where the practice is of being human.

Where the status quo is empathy, not fear.

A new nation whose supernatural beauty is beyond mere flesh and bones.

For all existence is birthed from the labour of Love of our great Mother.

Today, I call forth a nation.

Whose ebb flows with the energies of acceptance and respect.

Our potential to live in harmony with the land lays with our ability to live in harmony with each other.

To live!

Let live!

Harm no other!

Today, I call forth a nation.
Who is worthy of a better tomorrow, Now!
A people ready to fulfill their potential knowing the wisdom we seek
lays in our past when looked upon with Love.
The promise that is Turtle Island lies not perched on a pedestal for we are the pedestal of which her foundation is built.

Today, I call forth a nation.
Whose diversity of landscapes is reflected by the diversity of her people.
The dreams and hopes that is Canada fuels the warrior-poet to battle injustice with words of inclusion and equity.
Let us venture beyond time and space to see that the needs and wants of our ancestors do not differ from us today.
And the truth of their day, connects to the truth of our day,
for we are not separate from life. We are Life.
Let us dance, sing and rejoice as we reframe the

conditioning.

Let the light of our Love create a new affirmation of peace and prosperity.

Worry not of our legacy, for it will be written based on what we do Now.

And in this Now.

Let us remember the greatest of a country lies not in her government but with her people.

And as a people, let us be mindful, humble and inviting.

Be patient, kind, generous, gentle, joyous.

Choose to be of service!

Let us embrace this moment of Us!

Our native land is Mother Earth.

Oh, Canada, our chosen home.

We stand on guard for me, you, Us.

This is where we live!

Today, I call forth a new nation!

# Epilogue
by Dr. Diane Campeau, phD.

Vous avez lu les mots du poète qui s'inspire des forces suggestives du langage. Il sait marier le son et le sens, le rythme et la fluidité des mots. Sa poésie est une poésie engagée car à travers chaque phrase il nous livre à sa manière son avis sur des sujets qu'il juge important.

Je vous invite à rencontrer Rawle, l'homme derrière le poète et à écouter ses mots qui coulent comme une rivière, ou vous frappe comme une vague. Ce sont des mots qui nous provoquent dans un certain sens par une déclaration d'état d'urgence à la fois philosophique et poétique. Je vous propose d'avoir une discussion avec lui car la fin d'un poème n'est que le début d'un moment qui nous amène à nouveau ailleurs dans notre propre narration et qui nous rapproche tous de la même humanité.

*a poetic collection*

You have read the words of the poet. Those words inspired by the suggestive forces of the language. He knows how to marry the sound and the meaning, the rhythm and the fluidity of words. His poetry engaged us through every sentence and incite us to see his perspective on subjects he deems important.

I invite you to meet Rawle, the man behind the poet, and to listen to his voice that carries words that flow like a river or strikes you as a wave. He provokes us in a certain sense by a declaration of state of emergency both philosophical and poetic. After reading his poetry, I suggest you engage in a discussion with him, because the end of the poem is only the beginning of a moment that brings us further in our own narration and that gets us closer to our shared humanity.

## **TITLES**

1. It Matters Not
2. The Voice
3. Her Strength is Beauty
4. Blink into Existence
5. Iam is Me
6. Tumble-tumble
7. I Blink
8. Wild Child Free
9. Rhapsody in Choice
10. The Equinox of Change
11. Question and Answer
12. Broken Hearted Self
13. Naked
14. Tick-tock
15. Trapped

*a poetic collection*

16. Friendship Bound
17. Suspended Moment
18. Defined by Definition
19. Scared
20. Tao 'loading
21. When I Look
22. Necessary to You
23. Concrete, Glass, Asphalt and Cars
24. Grid Off
25. Me...You...Us
26. Two Fortnights
27. We Fight for Peace
28. Surrender's Ascension
29. Rainbow Culture
30. Calling Forth

## A FINAL WORD

Like others, I have many labels: father, son, brother, friend, poet. With all that I have achieved my greatest accomplishment is my kids: Harris, Zen and Irie. As much as I love all my roles, I am much more than those labels. I have fully embraced my purpose and walk by how to Love me and connecting to my worthiness. I no longer ask the question, who am I or why am I here for I am here to experience it all in the good graces of the universe.

I was born in Trinidad and Tobago to Agnes Toppin and Neville James. I have lived in Curepe, Brooklyn, Los Angeles, Washington, D.C., Toronto, Branford and Kelowna. I spent over 20 years in the corporate world in a variety of roles performing various tasks alongside good-hearted and well-intentioned people. The business world was my university where I learned how to exploit all my abilities in exchange for creating value for my employers. It was also in the corporate world, where my purpose first reared itself through managing people and creating strategies that would attract and retain individuals.

"I am evolution therefore I am always evolving."

*a poetic collection*

I am a community builder, facilitator, inspirational speaker, poet and transformation coach committed to enriching lives and building a community that is equitable, inclusive and respectful. My transformation from a victim mindset started when I heard a voice that asked a question, and the answer led to a door where walking through meant doing 'the work.' With the assistance of two amazing earth angels and surrendering to 'the work,' I unlocked my passion for being of service to our humanity.

Since moving to Kelowna, BC, I have had the good fortune of connecting to the community through my various roles and undertakings as a football coach, teacher, speaker, cultural animator, spiritual mentor, the various board of director positions as well as the founder of the Inspired Word Café (www.inspiredwordcafe.com).

I self-published my first book of poetry called "Truth Experienced" in 2012 and continue my work in human and community development through debunking the myth of race.

"My life is a beautiful balance of light and dark for without both there is no growth."

*In flow with* GRACE

*a poetic collection*

## ABOUT THE AUTHOR

Rawle James is an Inspirational Leader who has fully embraced his purpose to experience Love through the good graces of the Universe. He is the founder of the Inspired Word Café and self-published his first book of poetry called "Truth Experienced." His poetry inspires and challenges us to see love embodied within us. Rawle is committed to enriching lives and building a community that is equitable, inclusive and respectful.

Author Photo Credit: Bonita Kay Summers

www.ingramcontent.com/pod-product-compliance
Lightning Source LLC
Chambersburg PA
CBHW070622050426
42450CB00011B/3103